...and the fear
makes us special...

...and the fear
makes us special...

poems by
JOHN WING JR.

mosaic press

Canadian Cataloguing in Publication Data

Wing, John, 1949-
--and the fear makes us special

Poems.
ISBN 0-88962-725-8

I. Title.

PS8595.I5953A82 2000   C811'.54   C00-930743-5
PR9199.3.W49895A82 2000

Published by MOSAIC PRESS, P.O. Box 1032, Oakville, Ontario, L6J
5E9, Canada. Offices and warehouse at 1252 Speers Road, Units #1&2,
Oakville, Ontario, L6L 5N9, Canada and Mosaic Press, 4500 Witmer
Industrial Estates, PMB 145, Niagara Falls, NY 14305-1386

Mosaic Press acknowledges the assistance of the Canada Council, the
Ontario Arts Council and the Department of Canadian Heritage,
Government of Canada for their support of our publishing programme.

MOSAIC PRESS, in Canada:
1252 Speers Road, Units #1 & 2,
Oakville, Ontario, L6L 5N9
Phone / Fax: 905-825-2130
ORDERS:
mosaicpress@on.aibn.com
EDITORIAL:
cp507@freenet.toronto.on.ca

MOSAIC PRESS, in the USA:
4500 Witmer Industrial Estates
PMB 145, Niagara Falls,
NY 14305-1386 Tel:1-800-387-8992
ORDERS:
mosaicpress@on.aibn.com
EDITORIAL:
cp507@freenet.toronto.on.ca

Le Conseil des Arts | The Canada Council
du Canada | for the Arts

To Absent Friends:

Colin Campbell,

Tim Sims,

Gary David,

& Paul K. Willis

ACKNOWLEDGMENTS

Some of these poems appeared in different forms in *Vox Poetri*, *The University Of Windsor Review* and *Shecky Magazine*.

Thanks first and always to Howard Aster, a publisher most only find in their dreams.

Thanks to Michael Power, John Ditsky, Phil Hall, Anthony Wing, Paula Wing, and my wife, Dawn Greene, who read poems and drafts willingly (so they said) and offered excellent suggestions.

Thanks to my father, John M. Wing, who came to the train station and gave me $300 the day I left for Toronto, and has never stopped encouraging me to keep working and charge more.

Thanks to my mother, Angela Wing, who, early in my career, informed me that it was a "jungle" out there. And by God, she was right.

Thanks to Steve and Elaine Pulver.

Thanks to Dr Richard Meen.

And to the other women. Rachel Angela Brantley and Isabel Genevieve.

CONTENTS

THE COMEDIAN

NOTHING LIKE A CACTUS

I traveled thro' a land of men,
a land of men and women too.
And heard and saw such dreadful things
as cold earth wanderers never knew.

- William Blake

No one's interested in something you didn't do.

- Gordon Downie

One night in the early 1980's, a comedian went onstage at a well known New York comedy club. He was already a famous comedian who was always pushing the envelope, trying to find new ways of both irritating and entertaining an audience. The audience knew him and knew he would do something strange and outrageous. He began that evening by singing. He didn't say hello, *"How you guys' doin'?"*, he just went right into the song 100 BOTTLES OF BEER ON THE WALL. The audience giggled a bit for the first couple of minutes, but when he got to 89 bottles of beer, they were laughing loudly. The laughter continued through most of the 80's but began to seriously die out by 80 bottles. But the comedian didn't stop. The audience was not amused by the time he got to 70 bottles, and they were downright angry when he got to 60. Still he didn't stop. The audience began to yell and heckle but he soldiered on and on, seemingly oblivious to their displeasure. At 14 bottles of beer on the wall the comedian abruptly stopped and left the stage. The audience was stunned, and then angry again. They *called him back*. They screamed his name until he returned and sang the song to the end, finishing to wild applause. To Andy Kaufman, the audience was a wind-up toy.

I performed stand-up comedy on a club stage for the first time on June 30th, 1980. I went on something like fifteenth out of eighteen comedians on Amateur night at Yuk Yuks Comedy

Cabaret at Bay and Yorkville streets in Toronto. I was twenty years old, and had harboured a dream of being a comedian most of those years. Growing up in small town Canada, it was hard to convince myself that such a thing was possible to even try, much less something at which one could make a living.

I recall that evening quite clearly, possibly because my eight minute set went so well I could hardly believe it. It was akin to playing poker for the first time, knowing nothing, and cleaning out the veterans. The next time it went that well was almost three years later.

In late 1983, I embarked on a road trip that began my fifteen year odyssey of road work. Airport to airport, town to town, club to club, hotel to motel. I have performed in all ten provinces, 33 states, and over 400 cities and towns across the continent. In 1987, I worked fifty weeks out of fifty-two and forty-seven weeks out of town. It is a life that few who don't experience will ever understand. You work in bars, at night. You have more free time than anyone should ever be allowed, but it's ultimately quite punishing in its isolation and its temptations. I have tried here to give some understanding of my experience. I realize it is not definitive. It is only my view.

John Wing
15 April, 1999

the comedian

*"In high school, a teacher once said to me, 'Mike, do you think you're going to grow up and get a job where you can just tell **jokes** all day?'"*

- Mike MacDonald, Comedian

"I didn't come here to be laughed at, okay?"

- Tim Sims, Comedian

hair trigger

I had a bad temper;
irretrievable.

Tore out a boy's hair
in the schoolyard one day,
and they suddenly noticed.

Today they would say
I had "issues."

Sent a counselor
with long black hair
and a white streak up the middle
to talk to me.
She seemed nice,
and I did most of the talking.

Then she brought me into class,
stood me up in front of the board,
and the whole class, *in unison*,
said, "We love you, John."

As though what was missing
was the affection of my classmates.

I think of that moment, of wanting
to die in front of their gesture,
most nights, just before someone
calls my name, and I walk out
from behind a large curtain
to face once again
the verbal firing squad of love.

May 2-8, 1999
Tujunga, Calif.

audition

Clustered
like a school of sharks,
all alike. We hold scripts
and put meaning in our eyes.

Familiar faces
bring grins and bulltalk,
but eyes remain focused
on the door.

Each time it opens
a little more blood
runs out
and we smell it.

June 25, 1998
Studio City, Calif.

definitions

The comic
says
things funny

The comedian
says
funny things

The actor
speaks
another's words

The writer
cringes.

September 28, 1998
Toronto, Ont.

two lovers

The comedian is the unpublished street-poet of the stage.
The poet is on the page.

no   that's not it

The comedian wants to make you laugh.
The poet wants to make you think.

if you get it   wink

the comedian says funny things
the poet makes words sing

do it again

the comedian wants to be an actor
the poet wants to write novels

living in hovels

the comedian remembers everything that is said
the poet is good in bed

you are so deep

the comedian loves the sound of his voice
the poet loves sound

or is it the other way around?

one thing's sure
most die poor.

survival: 1980

In the summer of 1980, I played guitar at the corner of Wellesely and Yonge St in Toronto for cigarette and food money. One of the great things about street performing was that you didn't have to be any good at all. In fact, the worse you looked and played was more incentive for people to drop money into the case. And you only had to know one song. The foot traffic was so steady that no one ever hung around for much longer than a few bars, so you could stand there dressed in rags playing the same song over and over for four or five hours and make between ten and twenty dollars, which was enough in those days.

At the same time I was desperately pursuing a girl named Joan, who, it's easy to see now, was way out of my league. We met on a blind date, and she was frightened by my complete and instant infatuation. Looking back now, it was probably just a matter of her good taste. I wasn't what anyone would call handsome, and I made up for it with a total lack of charm. But I could not figure out her coolness. I was a comedian *and* a poet. I was young and strange looking, I had no job. What more could she want?

I would, often after an all night drug and bits session with other comedians, stop on my way home across from Wellesely subway station to try and catch a glimpse of Joan going to work. When I did see her, I would follow her. In those days they called it being lovesick. Today, I believe the term is stalking.

Of course, the corner I picked as my singing and begging place was a mere fifty feet from Wellesely station. I knew that one day she was bound to pass by. And she did. The fourth day I was there I saw her crossing Yonge St towards me, and when she got near me, I called out to her. I had really figured out the keys to making street money by then. So I was wearing an astoundingly filthy pair of ripped jeans, and this was ten or fifteen years before ripped jeans became fashionable. Back then they were an unmistakable sign of mental illness. I had a slightly torn, stained t-shirt that said Have A Shitty Day on it, and I was obviously unwashed and attempting a beard that looked more like clumps of dirt than hair.

Needless to say, Joan wasn't exactly thrilled to see me. When I said, "How're you doing?" I'm sure she had to fight off the urge to say, "Well, I have a life." She looked at me the way you'd look at a dead dog in the street. A mixture of pity and revulsion. "Are you *ok?*" she asked, obviously convinced of the answer. I told her I was doing fine, working amateur nights at Yuk Yuks, writing poems and sending them out. I said I'd even written a couple of poems about her. She just stood there shaking her head slightly, trying to define exactly what it was she was looking at. I told her I'd send her the poems and she said she was moving and would get me the new address. Funny, she never did. And, for as long as I played at that corner, she never passed by again. I assume she found a different route, or possibly even a different subway station.

I stopped writing love poems for her, and started writing jokes about her. Eventually I wrote a song about her, called "I Hope You Die." It became the triumphant closing piece of my act. Of course I didn't really want her to die. I wanted her to love me the way audiences eventually did whenever I sang that song.

amateur night

At first it was a week
between Mondays.

is this funny

Time to think up
a new personality.
An interesting, funny one.

it's in shy fun

And new jokes.
Opening with the only one
that worked last week.

fun tiny hiss

New clothing combinations.
I will always wear red
suspenders from now on.

shiny fit sun

Watching the pros
like a hawk. Asking why
about everything.

if shit sunny

The silence
teaching all
you'll ever need to know.

in fishy stun

August 15, 1998
Tujunga, Calif.

moving up

One night, still an amateur,
still toiling at a square job,
the best comedian
in Canada invited me (*me*)
to come to his place
after the show.

He had a ring of four
or five good comedians
who would go to his place
each night, smoke his dope,
and riff hundreds of new bits
which he would write down
& remember.

They were all stoned
and he was famous.

He came up to me,
in that I'm-going-to-speak-softly
-so-you'd-better-listen-hard
way of his, and said, "We're all
going to my place later to drop acid.
Wanna come?"

This was Zeus inviting a peasant to Olympus.
A comedian so funny that watching him made
you forget where, or who, you were.

And I had never dropped acid.

"I'd really like to," I said slowly.
"I really would. But I have to be
at work at nine a.m."
He grinned at me. The way
a wolf grins at a lamb.

"You'll *make it*," he said.

September 28, 1998
Toronto, Ont.

advice to a young comic

The night will come,
the comic said,
when no one laughs at all.

I've had those nights,
the amateur said,
when no one laughs at all.

But this night will be different,
said the comic,
with a knowing look.

The nights they laugh are different,
said another.
The nights they're silent are the same.

No, said the comic,
there'll be a night
when no one laughs at all.

And going home,
you'll realize,
they were *wrong*.

March 17, 1999
Tujunga Calif.

two shows only

The young comic went out there
in jeans and a sweater.
Said *fuck* till it was punctuation.
Gave them chapter and verse
of his sex life and drug life
and women and airplanes and cats.

That's my time, he intoned
as he finished. And now
here's your special guest.
Seen him on TV,
I know that you'll love him.
A big hand, how about it, come on.

The old guy came out all tuxedoed,
with his hair never moving, not once.
And he sang all the favourites,
did Cagney and Cooper, his face
an amusement park ride.
Not a word out of place,
not a gesture unknown.
They went nuts as he ended and bowed.

Between shows, the kid sat,
smoked a fat one. Had a beer
with his fingers and fries.
The old guy just paced
with his cigarette. Sipped water,
said little besides.

The kid finally said, Hey, relax man.
The next show's in an hour, sit down.
The comedian smiled, blew a smoke ring
and said, Can't sit down,
puts a crease in the suit.

March 17, 1999
Tujunga Calif.

deadheads: 1983

In the summer of 1983, I was booked as a middle act for a one nighter at the Tralfamadore, a jazz club in Buffalo. It paid the then incredible sum of $250. I had by then written a couple of funny songs and had brought the guitar back into the act. That turned out to be a lucky break.

The Tralf was an enormous room that held upwards of 600 people. There were 300 for our show. I did pretty well, and when I came off, the manager invited me to his office. Instead of paying me, He said, "We have Robert Hunter coming in tomorrow night and we'd like you to stay over and open for him. It's two shows, and we'll pay you $100." My reply still amazes me. "I'd love to," I said, "but why is it I'm worth $250 tonight for one show and only $100 tomorrow for two shows?" There was a moment of residual terror before he said, "You're right. You're absolutely right. We'll pay you $250." We shook on it and I left walking on air.

Robert Hunter was the longtime lyricist for the Grateful Dead, and a really nice guy to boot. The club was packed to the rafters with Deadheads. It was my first experience opening for anyone and one of the largest crowds I had ever performed for. At show time, the announcer came out and screamed, *"ARE YOU READY FOR ROBERT HUNTER!?!"* An enormous cheer shook the room. *"OKAY, BUT FIRST, HERE'S THE COMEDY OF JOHN WING!!!"* Instead of another cheer, there was a loud groan, followed by some polite applause. I went out and did all right. I noticed that the drug jokes seemed to get the best response. Then I went to the bar and watched Robert's show. He was very good and the Deadheads adored him.

Between shows, I hung out with Robert in his dressing room. He produced two powerful joints, which we smoked, and he taught me some guitar licks. I was having a lot of fun, and I went out for the second show feeling my oats. I wasn't on more than a minute before I realized they hadn't turned the crowd. It was the same stoned 600 people who'd seen me three hours earlier. They were yelling out my punch lines and getting quite loud, and I had twenty minutes to do and no act, since I didn't have much more than the twenty I'd done the first show.

Without thinking too much about it, I picked up my guitar and called for requests. Several artist's names were called out and I picked one – Bob Dylan. I sang "You Ain't Going Nowhere" and they seemed to like it. So I picked out another from the calls and did a second song, then a third, and a fourth. They were getting into it, but I felt it was dragging. I needed to do something up tempo to get them going. So when I finished the fourth song I went straight into "Good Lovin" by the Rascals. The audience went mildly berserk at my choice. They cheered, whistled, stamped their feet, and sang along. The feeling of power was truly remarkable. I finished the song to wild applause, did one more, and said goodnight, enormously relieved that I had gotten through it. They called me back for an encore. The first one I'd ever received. I sang "Sweet Baby James" and got off on a cloud. Robert asked me how I knew to sing "Good Lovin". It turned out the Grateful Dead performed that song at all their shows. Lucky.

To this day I still have it on my résumé that I opened for the Grateful Dead. If anyone asks, I say, "In Buffalo. 1983."

the comedian

This is what I chose,
not knowing at the moment
of choice what would come.
Knowing only the bone-quaking
thrill of the sound.

It comes like a warm wave.
Surrounding, then retreating.
Then comes the chase.
I was 13 when I first felt it.
20 when I caught it again.

Choosing to pursue the sound
leads to the road, the towns,
the hotels and motels,
the days open and unslept,
and the waiting.

The road is two things:
the large truth of the traveler.
The driving days, the flying days.
The there and back and there again
and back again. And also the way
you come to know towns, which
really isn't any way at all.

You only know the road in
to the gig and the road back
to the highway afterward.
People ask if you've been to this
town or that town and you say yes.
Lying, because you haven't been
to a town, but only to a road.
The hotel is your hope, the motel
your reality. You know their shape,
their colour, the size and smell
of all that free soap. You could find
the ice machine blind because you know
the noise it makes.

And the days, all that time
to spend money or read or sleep,
lapping the channels until you're sure,
masturbating until you've hurt yourself,
wondering what the maid will think,
waiting for sundown.

The night comes, and it dresses you.
You like darkness all around
and only you in the light.
This is your hour to be alive.
This is your longshort speech, your plea.
And the sound fills you like a sail.

That is what I chose.
The inexplicable life. The unshared
moment when I hear my being
dance.

Where my most intimate thoughts
are related to the faceless,
and music is the laughter
I rip from them.

Hard to explain.
Most think it's the applause,
but it's not.
Applause signals the end.
Time to go, show's over.
Get the car, reverse the turn,
find the road to the highway
to the next road, and the soothing
blackness of night driving.

The sound still running through my head
like blood.

February 25-April 6, 1998

inside joke

How many comedians
does it take
to change a light bulb?

Four.

One to change the bulb,
And three to say, "That's funny."

Three.

One the change it,
and two to say, "My way's funnier."

Two.

One to change it,
and one to say, "He stole that from me."

One

to say, "Listen, don't do your light bulb bit, okay?
Cause I want to do my light bulb bit, and if you
do yours before me, mine'll get nothing."

Zero.

August 18-24, 1998
Tujunga, Calif.

"Cold foot on the pedal, cold hands on the wheel."

- John Newlove

star crossing

Two hours from home
the road curved without me.
The sound jerked me back,
darkness to dark.

Pounding heart reminded me
to pay attention.
Her voice had taken my eyes.
What she couldn't say.

Love had become a debate
with myself. While driving
I could scream at her
tiptoed caution.

But the skid and screech
of tires brought back
the truth of the black road.
Nothing is concealed.

Deep down she knows.
If she needs me,
I'll be in my car
somewhere.

Winter 1987-Summer 1998

poem/joke

Breaking Up:

She said it was too much.
The way I loved her. She felt
too confined in my enthusiasm.

I said I would do anything
to keep her affection chained
to my soul. Then I begged

for another chance, my eyes
locked with hers, afraid if I turned
away for even a moment–

Then came screaming, tears,
resentment, recrimination, fear,
and the sound of the door.

Onstage, two nights later,
I said:

"She said I was too intense,
so I stared at her until she cried."

September 28, 1998
Toronto, Ont.

showcase

I'm going *first*?
Why do I always have to go first
every damn showcase? They won't even
remember me, for Christ's sake.
Who's hosting? *Him*? Jesus, make it
as tough as they can...he *never*
gets laughs off the top. They'll
be colder than shit when I get out there.
Should I open with the sex thing?
You know, the I-never-have-sex
and this is why blah blah, you know it.
Bull*shit* you wrote it! Are they starting?
Is the guy even here yet? My luck he'll
be late. They're always late. He won't
even *see* my set and – hey he got a laugh.
Which joke was it? That one? Christ,
that means they're stupid. They'll never get
my stuff. I'll spend the whole set over their heads.
Why do I *always* have to go first?
Is that his wrap up? Is he wrapping up?
How long's he been up there, anyway?
Why doesn't he introduce me? I hate him.
I'm gonna open with the sex thing.
Okay, here we go. Get ready.
Fuck.

October 1, 1998
Tujunga, Calif.

small world: 1988

In 1987 I worked 50 weeks: 47 weeks out of town, two weeks in town, and one week as an actor. I performed in all ten provinces and six U.S. states. I had a good year. I even met my future wife, a talented, well endowed comedian from Los Angeles. By the end of the year, we were in love, and after some discussion of whether she should move to Toronto or I should move to L.A., we decided I would move to Los Angeles. I planned a long western road trip for the early part of 1988. Starting in Winnipeg in February, I would continue to Vancouver and find my way to L.A. from there.

But the decision nagged at me. I had always said I wouldn't leave Canada. Why did I suddenly want to now? In Toronto I was a big fish; one of the best comedians in the country. In L.A., as my wife-to-be so charmingly put it, I would be plankton. Even as I was giving notice to my landlord, and divesting myself of the accumulated possessions of eight years, I still wasn't sure.

The last night I spent in Toronto, I went out rather than hang around in my now bare apartment. Yuk Yuks had opened a new club on Queen Street, and I wanted to check it out. It was a cozy little room, and the show was called "Girl's Night Out." It featured only women comedians. I stood in the back and the first person I noticed was an actress I had dated a few months back. She performed in a nude musical and I had taken her out twice and slept with her once. It hadn't gone well. She was sitting at a table with another actress I had dated for several months. Our breakup had been bitter and she now hated the mere sight of me. I moved to the far corner of the room.

From the shadows I spotted a reporter from the *Toronto Sun* who had interviewed me once. The interview had gone very well, and after the article had come out, I asked her out to celebrate. We ended up in bed that night, and that had not gone well. It was a good thing I'd waited until the article appeared. At the table next to the reporter was a woman who was a personal manager. I had slept with her once, many years before. The fact that I didn't sleep with her again may suggest a pattern. Then a comedian was introduced. I'd dated her for six weeks about three years earlier, until she faked a pregnancy to help me "get my priorities straight." I stood there, truly astounded at what I'd blundered into. The woman finished and went out into the audience, seating herself at the table of the personal manager I'd slept with. It was becoming eye-glazingly surreal.

The next comedian to be introduced was a lesbian whom I'd fallen for the previous year. I'd made a big play for her, not realizing her orientation, and actually got her into bed once. To say it hadn't gone well would not tell the full story. Perhaps she wasn't completely sure about her sexuality. After sleeping with me, she was sure.

While I watched her perform, I began to count the audience members. There were sixty people in the room, including comedians. One tenth of the crowd were ex-lovers of mine. In a city of over 3 million people, *six* women I had slept with had gathered in one place. Moving to Los Angeles began to look like the right decision after all. I'd only slept with one woman there. The woman I would eventually marry. We were in love, and she was willing to overlook the fact that it hadn't gone well.

biograph

I dated a famous lesbian
once, for as long
as it took to remove
her doubt.

I slept with a submissive man
once. We canceled
each other out
like integers.

I got married
once, several years
before I became
a husband.

I experimented with drugs
once, for as long
as I can't remember.

I said I would never
leave my country.

I left my country,
and said I would never
return.

June 1, 1998
Tujunga, Calif.

nightshift

What it feels like, I suppose,
is magic.
An electroding search
for sound-gulfs
and brain explosions.

You stand there talking,
making faces, (you have
no real idea what the faces look like,
just the knowledge that when
your face does *this* on *that* word,
the laugh's bigger) and moving
in a small circle, one hand
in pocket, one hand holding
the mike, elbow crooked
into the ribs, so the mike moves
everywhere you do.

You recite the novel.
The stories that begin true
and end in absurd lies,
but like the faith of the guilty,
you believe what you're saying,
finding the truth of your life
in these performed fabrications.

And you produce no tables
or chairs, no steel beams
or stained glass. Only laughter.
Sudden involuntary agreement-sounds
that windmill you up, charging you
even as you time them.

You are inside and outside
yourself while your mind hurricanes
ahead, storing and suggesting.

It makes you invincible.
For that hour each day,
high above it all. A full moon
floating, creating the tide.

interview

Asking
(*she looks at her notes*)
about *why* someone
would *want* to do comedy,
she speaks of the nudity
of the soul
out there with the black
wall and the white light;
the knowledge of silence
and its ramifications.

(*she actually uses this word*)

My eyebrow must be doing something
disbelieving so she admits
that she is much too insecure
to *ever* do what I do.

I smile,
(*and so does she, realizing
she's hit it bang on*)

If you would never – could
never – do it, I begin,

(*her pen flies to spill this thought as it comes*)

it means
you're not insecure
enough.

September 28, 1998
Toronto, Ont.

making friends

Afterwards,
when you're sitting
at the back of the room,
breathing in the air
of a finished performance,
they come to you with smiles
so sweet they drip on you.

Your face is relaxed
after its hour of shining
concentration, and their eyes
acupuncture your cheeks,
forcing the wonder
of what it means
on your smile back.

Most just passionately
want to tell you
how they laughed,
thank you for what you do.
Others have a definite subtext
in the repeated phrase,
"You were *great*."

And afterwards,
after sex, they say
"You're *funny*."

October 11, 1998
Calgary, Alta.

the tonight show

Studied ten years for this
six minute exam,
with everything riding.

Flown and driven thousands
of miles and cities to come
to this place.

Standing behind a curtain,
thinking – *walk slowly* –
with everything riding.

Notes in my pocket,
memorized until they make me gag.
Go slow – hit the mark –

The talent coordinator smiles,
hand on the curtain,
with everything riding.

Staring at the curtain,
where the hole will be
when my name is called.

Pounding in my chest,
thinking, *don't have a heart attack*
with everything riding.

Walk slow – go slow
– hit the mark – you've done
*this – you've **done** this.*

Pulling the curtain open,
he turns to me and says,
'*Don't forget your jokes.*'

October 12, 1998
Calgary, Alta.

the art of the spin: 1986

Shawn Thompson was a comedian of rare ability. He was criminally handsome, with blond locks almost as shiny as his teeth. He could play the guitar and sing, he did some sleight-of-hand, he worked with props, and he could handle virtually any audience or situation. And he never bombed. *Never.* I watched him perform everywhere for six years before I saw him do anything but a great show. He didn't have great material, but he had presence and a belief in himself, a quick wit, and he knew every trick in the book. Find a male audience member early in the show, and make fun of him exclusively the whole night. When heckled, be fast. If you need time, repeat what the heckler said. If the heckler gets a big laugh, that means extra time for you, and you can time your riposte off the laugh. And on and on. Nothing ever fazed Shawn.

I got to see one of his big tricks close up the second time I ever went to Yuk Yuks. It was a Saturday night, I was alone, and was placed near the front. Shawn found me there, asked me a few questions, getting laughs off all of my answers, then asked me onstage. Once there he had me give him my wallet, ostensibly so he could do a magic trick with some money. As he took the wallet he slipped something into it. I saw it, but the audience didn't. Then, while searching for money and complaining that there was none, he came upon something that made him laugh. He turned to the crowd and said, "I've had a lot of wallets up here, but this is the first time I've ever found *anything* like this..." whereupon he pulled a condom (in its packet) out of the wallet, giggling as though it was the funniest thing he'd ever seen. Then he stepped across the tables to shake hands with the woman I was sitting with. Of course it caused a sensation. This was in 1980, mind you. I doubt it would cause much of a sensation today.

In the next six years I saw Shawn do the condom bit probably three or four hundred times. It never failed him. Until one night in 1986.

It was Amateur Night, and as usual there were fifteen or sixteen hopefuls waiting in the green room. It was going to be a long show. Shawn was hosting, which meant it was going to be a very long show, because he would do his whole act, in pieces, before it was all over. There were four or five professional comics in the back of the room watching the show, chatting, and periodically going out to get high. As the show wore on, there wasn't anyone that interesting on so we stopped paying attention. We had just come back in after smoking a joint when Shawn came out and decided to do the condom bit for the loud and raucous Monday night crowd, many of whom were regulars. He picked out a Goober from Gooberville for the trick, a guy with fewer teeth than he had nostrils and eyebrows combined. The guy got up, handed over the wallet, and the trick played out as always. However, after Shawn found the condom, and as he was walking over to congratulate the Goober's girlfriend, the guy grabbed the wallet away from Shawn, went to the mike and said, "He planted that one." Then he reached into the wallet, pulled out another condom, and said, "This one's mine."

I don't recall how the audience felt about it, because we were laughing so hard we couldn't hear anything. Shawn wasn't fazed, of course. He never was. He said, "You should thank me, you prick." The bit had never failed, but on the extraordinarily off chance that it might, he had a line ready. You don't have to know how to dance, but you do have to know how to spin.

chief

(For Colin)

<u>I</u>

Death

questions the living.

<u>II</u>

Those of us
who survived
speak of you often.

You just walked away one day
and they found you
three months later.

You might have fallen,
jumped, or just
fell asleep or passed out.

In the wrong place
on the wrong night
or the right place
on the right night.

They used dental records
to identify you.
You were 33.

III

They called you *Chief*.
And speaking of you now,
it is the only name we use.

Some who came after ask,
Why Chief?
Because he was the best?

We nod, not wishing
to say the real reason.
Because you were the best.

And it's not politically correct
anymore to say
he drank like an Indian.

IV

When you first started
performing, you were
so shy that you looked
at the floor and mumbled
your jokes.

Some have raided
your vast catalogue
and do your material now
as their own.

When we hear it,
all we can do is look
at the floor
and mumble.

V

I remember you
arriving back at the hotel
one morning at 6:50,
drunk, probably glad
that woman declined
your kind offer.

Seated on your bed,
suddenly realizing
you had a radio show
at 7:30, you called
the front desk and asked
for a wake up call
at 7:00.

The clerk, flabbergasted,
said, "But sir, it's 6:58 now."

And you said,
"You'd best be dialing."

VI

We once agreed,
you and I, at 3am
somewhere,
that this was a great way
to spend our twenties.

And we spent them
like money.

VII

I miss you.
I suppose the police don't
much anymore.

When we gather now and tell
the new guys your stories
the number of cops you took on
that rainy night in West Van
is multiplied.

I usually say
it was nine.

VIII

I always wanted to ask you
what it was like to wake up
or, in your case,
regain consciousness
in a straitjacket.
Wondering
am I paralyzed?

Recalling nothing.

IX

The last time
we worked together
was that one-nighter
in Vernon. The one
with the hotel
that had a river
in the lobby.

You were taking pills
for your back. On
the wagon, you said proudly.
"Fifty-one and a half more
weeks and it'll be a year."

X

I'm sober almost
four years now.

And lucky.

I think sometimes
of the last time I saw you.
Was there something
in the story that night?

Something your eyes
were telling me?

Could I have altered
the course of your
medicated pageant,
or turned back
the cluster-fuck of time?

June 20-24, 1998
Tujunga, Calif.

life italicized

...and the fear makes us special...

The polls say
the majority's greatest fear
is standing up and speaking
in front of people.

And we, the conquerors
of this fear, are frightened
of the morning, of going
to the same place
at the same time
every day,
every year.

We want our same places
to be different
from you who fear standing
and talking. Our same
places are in different towns
and hotels and clubs where
different people come each night.
We love the night.

And the fear makes us special.
The fear we have of silence;
of not being
liked or even noticed.

And the job, too.
Unless you've done it,
we say, unless you've been
up there gutting your self
for the loud pleasure
of people you will never know,
you will never really know.

How we ridiculously assume
accountants and programmers,
horse trainers and hookers don't
feel the same. That ours
is the life italicized.

They fear standing and talking,
but also, like us, the great fright
is just being
the same.

And the fear reminds us
to avoid being
like everyone.
O r someone.

October 16, 1998
Edmonton, Alta.

the more things change: 1994

Forty years of timing the lightning doesn't change what you are the moment you step back into the darkness.

In the spring of 1994, I happened to be at the Tonight Show studio one afternoon taping a different show, and I was invited to stay and watch Jay and his guests from the producer's well. The main guest that night was Don Rickles, whom I had never seen live, and although I never cared too much for his style of comedy, I wanted to see him and possibly meet him.

I watched Don Rickles that night, a man easily in his mid sixties, a comedian for over forty years. He came out, sat down with Jay, and just murdered. Big laughs all through his segment. He was sweating profusely but never working hard for the laugh. Just laying out his attitude and punching every line. They went to commercial on a huge, bring-down-the-house kind of laugh, and brought out a new guest after the break. A minute into her interview, Rickles jumped in and killed all over again making fun of everything the lady and Jay were saying. After the musical guest, they came back for the sign off. Don did one last joke, getting another big laugh as the show closed.

After the sign off, Jay came around the desk and I was standing close by when he said to Don, "Just great. Just fantastic. Thank you so much for coming." They shook hands and Don came down towards where I was. I was about to congratulate him myself when the director and producer grabbed him, showered him with accolades, which he took very humbly, with a tired smile. Then a woman came up to him and introduced her little daughter to the great Mr. Rickles. He smiled at the child, thanked the woman, who was also full of grand praise, and moved to the corridor that led to the dressing rooms. I followed him fairly closely, but he never turned around.

When he got to his dressing room, his manager, a wizened little man, was waiting with a broad smile and an outstretched hand. Don reached for the hand and the little man said, "Way to go." Don gave the man a piercing look and said, "It was ok? Really? It was *really* ok?" The man smiled again. "It was great," he said. "It was?" Don replied. "It really was *good*?" The man nodded, and they disappeared inside, closing the door.

true story

A man who lived underneath love
was walking from nowhere to nowhere
soaked by imagined rain

His life strolled beside him
unnoticed

The only voice he heard
was invented for him

Below the skin-cylinder
he was all wires

And he walked
through the night of his sun
and the rain of his day
all the way
to nowhere

And the blue-black sky
tried to catch his eye
to say – this is only –

and it was

October 26, 1998
Mexico City

elegy for paul

His death came
unfanfared, unimagined,
and unbelieved.

His wicked smile
would not have stooped
to such an exit.

Teeth bared,
he alone of us all
could force the end
to back away,
heaving in pained laughter,
calling *stop*,
asking *please*.

One assumes
he has merely moved on
to a larger audience
in an uncensored palace.

They will at first not know
their luck,
and be wary of this panther,
but will certainly
come to appreciate him
later
and in all time.

November 25, 1999
Caribbean Sea

ethics: 1982

Recently fired from my straight job, about to go on unemployment for the first time, and not really going anywhere as a comedian, an opportunity presented itself. I was hanging around with Mike MacDonald's crew of guys in the spring of 1982. Four guys I played poker with, smoked dope with, wrote and complained with. They were the four regular hosts at Yuk Yuks. At the time, other than headlining, hosting was the only paying spot at the club. It paid the princely sum of twenty-five dollars a show. And there were other benefits. It led to headlining. Become a middle act and you could die a middle act. Hosting taught you the tricks. How to handle the crowd, how to deal with hecklers, how to be funny in any situation, how to keep the show moving. And it forced you to write new material because you couldn't just do your act, and even when you did, the audience was riddled with regulars who had seen you many times and were likely to yell out punch lines before you got to them. Everyone wanted to host but Mike's four minions had it locked up.

One day, smoking hash at one of the guys' basement hovels, they concocted a plan to strike because the club owner flatly refused to raise the hosting fee. They made two mistakes. One was believing that a show of solidarity would frighten the owner, and the second one was to discuss the plan with me in the room. Stoned as I was, what I had to do was as plain as the seven fingers on the hand I was intently studying. So, they struck, informing the owner that they wouldn't host or perform at the club again until he doubled the money. They told him on a Monday, after they had booked all the hosting spots for the week. That afternoon, I presented myself to the owner and said, "Gee, I'd love to host." I was quickly booked, and became a host.

I wasn't the only guy who crossed the line. I was just the only friend of theirs who did so. The so-called strike lasted all of a week, although the four of them didn't host again for three months, the penalty for disloyalty. Within two years, I was one of the top hosts in the country. Hosting was even more of a ticket than I thought. I worked the Ottawa club something like 28 times in two and a half years. As a headliner or middle act, the best one could hope for was twice, possibly three times a year. The price of what I did was the friendship of four other comedians. The benefit was immeasurable.

Yes, I stabbed my comrades in the back. And looking back on it, all I can say is, fuck 'em. This job has never been about organizing, about solidarity between colleagues. It's about me. I sell me. I degrade myself, lick boots, kiss ass, get screwed in order to further my career, not yours. The lesson was: Never linger over a dead comrade. Step up smartly and say, "Hey, I guess you'll be needing someone to replace him on all those gigs he had booked." Because they will need someone. And it might as well be me.

drove all night

Standing
outside the Comedy Store
on Sunset Boulevard
in 1987.

Staying at the hotel next door.
Looking huge-eyed
at everything.

Paid 7 dollars
and sat down. The host
introduced Richard Pryor.
I looked at my watch.
I had been in Los Angeles
a little more than an hour.

Now
12 years late
for the sitcom, the movie.
Behind the club, could see
the show for free, but I'm outside
where the lights flash in a line.
Dice's ranting voice yelling
"*Fuck.*" The word slips
out the door and dissipates
in the parking lot
like a sparkler.

Thinking
of bearded Lenny,
dead, posed naked
on the bathroom floor,
being filmed
for a future "*Say No To Drugs*" video.

His name a ghost.
Nobody really remembers.
The crazy one – laughing
at judges, naming cops,
(shouldn't have done *that*)
retreating into the needle,
suffocating until it spat him out.
Naked. Dead. On film.

Not about what we can say now,
or even
what we can't say.

Nobody's laughing anymore anyway,
They say, *"Right on,"* or they applaud.
They don't know who died for our
tits-on-the-radio rights.
Neither do we.

Drunk on bitterness, on
the injustice of Richard in the wheelchair
smiling as though you're going
to buy him ice cream,
and then feed it to him through a straw.

Time to go home.
When they're older
I'll tell them,
that I was here. (*there*)
I bought the albums, the drugs,
the whole story.

Drove all night,
all the way home in a blizzard.
Drove all night
and they never paid me.

Did the *Tonight* Show
with the guy before Leno.
Rode a white stretch limo,
long as this room,
into L.A. that night
and saw Richard Pryor
live
for 7 bucks.

October 28-November 2, 1999
Hollywood, Calif.

nothing like a cactus

He invented a rainbow but lightning struck it

- Earle Birney

She fell in love, you see, with someone that I used to be.

- Tom Waits

obloquy

don't read enough

don't understand

the simple curvature

of spinal dignity

don't see until

years later

playing incidents

again & again

& finally something

clicks in

the way he said it

the way he looked

the undeciphered smell

I can't bring back

but know now was

alcohol

June 6, 1998
Tujunga, Calif.

a theory

To be a parent

is to be cruel

mistaken

under funded

callous

hearthroated

ragingly

idiotic

swearing

never again

what you once

swore

never

June 6, 1998
Tujunga, Calif.

tall tale

I rejected my country,
but not what it taught me.

Something pushed me away,
family, ego, money, the same
old wintry things.

I return the exotic one to some,
the long lost boy who lives
way out there

where the sun shines every day
and the people are crazy for guns
and drugged to deepen their intrinsic
shallowness.

To me it's merely a town built for cars
instead of people.
A company town.

Glamour is a place you haven't been.

June 13, 1998
Tujunga, Calif.

out of the woods

I've seen the last elm tree in Canada
somewhere between Ottawa and Cornwall
standing proud at the edge of a cornfield

One of those, "quiet trees"
content in its own company
grown apart

Alone since the epidemic swept through
somehow the germ missed this one

Must be laughing at the alders
always saying "stay with the group
don't get separated"

Diseases are thorough
like rebels
the resistant strains

No one thought they'd *all* perish
they were only trees after all

The government will nail a plaque to it someday
This is the last elm tree in Canada
Do not climb

June 15, 1998
Tujunga, Calif.

first cracks

You said
You only touch me
to feel yourself;
to know you're there.

Offhandedly,
a snatch of conversation.

But it stayed in the house.

Every morning, waking
and groping my way
into the kitchen
to start the coffee,

it was there.

And I would wonder,
how many times
have I done this?

Had the mornings
and nights of the years
blurred into a Ferris wheel
ride, where every image
is anticipated
correctly?

Bringing you your cup
I would wait a moment
before waking you, and stroke
your arm.

Understanding
nothing
but the presence
of my fingers.

June 25-27, 1998
Studio City, Calif.

to everything

That spring,
she went around the neighbourhood
distributing flyers
that predicted the apocalypse
to the same people to whom
he was trying to sell insurance.

In the fall,
she stopped eating
everything except fruit.

Their second child, a girl,
was born as the first
snow fell.

She hated his job.
Refused to find one herself.

The children remained
in day care.

All winter
she searched for the perfect religion.
Discovering a flock
of communal doomsayers
in Arizona.

When spring
came around again
they were apart,
the goods divided.

He got the children.
She got the fruit
and the end of the world.

July 9, 1998
Tujunga, Calif.

outdoor sports

The women pass
in white and red.
My thick book blurs,
is left unread.

They cross my bridge,
they shift my gears.
The women glide
around my ears.

The women pass
like butterflies.
Their gleaming scent
fills up my eyes.

Each woman is
a brand new page
Shameful really,
at my age.

In open secret
every night,
I call them up
in kilobyte

The women stroll
without a care.
They coat my dreams,
and bruise my air.

July 19-August 15, 1998
Tujunga, Calif.

to where you lead
(*For Dawn*)

I grew up with elbows
and clenched hearts.
Cried a lot, hated
myself for not being...

I have a photo of you
from that first week
ten years ago.
Your hand is on your shoulder.

Your smile is a beckoning.
A sort of *'Are you coming?'* smile.
'I'm already here.' You seem
to say. *'Join me.'*

I grew into fingers
and the soft tongues of your love.
Stumbled, sin-racked
into your forgiveness.

And there is no darkness
in your open hand, posed lightly
on our strange beginning,
your knowing eyes following me

to where you lead.

July 19, 1998
Tujunga, Calif.

desert bloom

Love is nothing like a cactus
thriving in the sun
the thick skin protecting
all that juice

Love has no spine-armour
to ward off the territorially
impaired

Love dries in the constant sun,
becomes brittle
easily snapped or shredded

The cactus flower comes
once a decade
an atomic blast of colour and fire,
as if to say
you don't know me.

Love can flower and die
in a day,
an hour
a moment
and bloom again immediately

Love is insecure
slow-witted
internalized only
for the moment of realization,
no instinct for survival
it burns out

The cactus grows tall and green
without predator
insult
or infidelity
saving rain for a sunny day.

July 9-18, 1998
Tujunga, Calif.

dogwalk

The two go running
up the dirt path lined with dogfences
ahead of me, and I call
but like milkmen they know
where to stop. Each enclosure
is a dog or two. The old collie's first,
although she never even comes limping
to the chainlink anymore, despite their calls.

Sucking on sweet grass, the two
are off to the huskies' compound,
singing the names of the pure white
and black year-olds, who tear at the bars
and leap with their tongues at the two
who pet and scratch them hello.
Next is the golden retriever, who has heard
us coming and waits expectantly, pawing the ground.

Sometimes we head up the vacant hill
by the stone bed where the rain cut a river
last year, and the two forage for shiny plastic
or the turquoise tossed from old fishtanks.
One looks for rattlesnakes, and the other
stands on the bear-shaped rock, throwing
her arms above my falling fear,
forever queen of the bird trails.

Then slipslide down the last unpaved path
to the turning, where one visits the dogs
by the tarp-draped fence, and the other
strokes a black cat across the narrow way.
Past the unseen pit bull and loud Chihuahua,
they play wirewalkers on the small brick wall
as I hold their hands, then jump to the gravel
of the last house, calling out the Maltese.

A chat with the white hair, a few foraged pebbles,
and it's back to the drag, looking both ways
and facing the traffic for the unsidewalked final leg.
The two ask for a trip to the licorice store, and run
ahead to the steps laughing, calling leaders and winners.
Past the flowers, the juiceless sweetgrass littering their wake,
to the door they cannot open, and so call to me
and I arrive, in last place, my pockets full of stones.

September 17, 1998
Tujunga, Calif.

symptoms

Sitting next to a toilet with my child,
watching and applauding the new learned
function.

I am 39 now.

Still bathmaster to one daughter.
Shooed out by the other
who has discovered privacy.

I listen to talk radio.

Asking a teacher why poor spelling
was not corrected on homework,
she replies, "We don't do that anymore."

It's all up to me.

Celebrate four years of sobriety
by going out, not drinking,
and losing my chequebook.

It wasn't like this when I was young.

Removing my hat after a workout,
I note that the sweatband smells
just like my father.

September 17-18, 1998
Studio City/Tujunga, Calif.

legacies

From my wife
they will inherit
love, of course,
& patience.
The understanding
that perfection
is the goal,
a prescience
about plotlines,
& nice breasts.

From me they'll get
dark hair,
myopia,
a flashpaper temper,
addiction,
egocentrism,
low self-esteem,
procrastination,
homosexual tendencies,
& Catholicism.

September 23-October 6, 1998
Toronto-Calgary

harbour lights

Last night I dreamt about you,
Marilyn Bell.

And you swam,
hour after hour, stopping
to tread water and be fed
or rubbed with another layer
of raw lanolin, then on again,
stroke after stroke,
wave after wave
slapping your face,
across Lake Ontario
during that crazy summer
five years before I was born.

You were 16.
With Gus, your coach
in the follow boat.

The water was so cold
that it numbed you
into unconsciousness
for the last two hours.

You awoke near the Toronto shore
after almost 21 hours,
and you saw the lights blinking
And there were people
hundreds of them
who watched you stand
and walk to the beach
and how they cheered you.

A teenager.
You were the first across,
doing something no one had ever done,
and many said could never be done.

And all day I've been thinking of you,
Marilyn Bell.

Swimming across Lake Ontario
before you could vote.

Maybe because I'm almost forty now.
Maybe because I wish
I could have been there that night
on the beach, cheering you.

Maybe because I wonder
if I'll see the harbour lights
and they'll come to me with blankets
when I awake
and see the shore.

August 31, 1998
Tujunga, Calif.

aeropuerto, mexico

I

Flying into the Mexico City
aeropuerto.

Wondering what the first person
who saw this valley
would think of it now,
all raftered in corrugation.
A crumbling urbanity
stretching as far
as the eye can imagine.

From the sky,
the green taxis
look like lawns
in search of empty yards.

II

teal-blue tiled ceiling
half suspended

girl with a belly button
& bad shoes

amoeba phones
opening to receive

we are crushed by paper
& burn for trees

sun behind
a cloud-river
like a hospital
window
the people who live
out there

are cured

October 26, 1998
Mexico City

st. boniface cemetery winnipeg, 1985

By the snow-banked Assiniboine,
so cold you can't feel your hand
in front of your face, fresh flowers,
garlands, bouquets, rainbows
of roses on a perfectly swept
grave.

Funny how we, the interlopers,
the third coming of history,
want to write about Riel.
As though our insight into
our not-so-great great grandparents'
decisions means anything now.

Frozen rock-snow everywhere
except this corner. Room enough
for six graves. But only one
monument, chimney-shaped.
The name cries out. One name,
one year, one hundred years ago.

Could say they were frightened
by his strength, galvanized to murder
by his appeal. But who among
the lucky descendants of conqueror
whites even cares now? We honour
no one, save the Jesus we kill for.

October 12, 1998
Calgary, Alta.

foreign affair

My brother buys
toilet paper in Hong Kong.
Disdaining the twelve pack.
"I won't be here that long'.
The Cantonese salesgirl's eyes
widen at the one finger he signs back.

My brother finds
moments of great intimacy
in encounters like this.
In private jokes and history
with servicepeople of all kinds
and he recalls each one, like a kiss.

My brother makes
her laugh and even thinks
he'll make her understand
his prudence, as she blinks
and nods. She's known flakes,
but none like this strange, constipated man.

July 19, 1998
Tujunga, Calif.

hearing she had married

Not under you;
not elbowed out of vision's
sweep, nor transfixed in your
time-lapse brain, still young
and voice-cracked, lost and found.

Not over you;
not speckled with your virus
still, nor all awake with
wondering. The hows
and whys have taken place.

Not long ago,
not still alone or even
sad, I heard you speak
discovery, the golden
heart raised from the stream.

Not simply so;
not smarting each from separate
perch, nor longing souls in
atrophy. Not over
you. Not yet. Not me.

September 17, 1998
Studio City/Tujunga, Calif.

and god said

And God said, Let there be light. And there was light.
And God was lonely, resting on the seventh day,
He was so lonely. So God said,
Let there be cable, and there was cable.
Let there be DirecTV and PrimeStar
and Pay-Per-View so that my children
will have something to watch while worshiping me.
Let there be ratings and newsmagazines and scandal
and tabloids and ragtime and rap and Spam. Let the
    people
taste this Spam, and resolve never to touch it again,
for it is unclean. Let there be food for some
and none for others. Let one percent
of the people own 90% of the wealth
and let the rest have me for their comfort.
And God said, Let the good times roll

Let there be the Spice Girls and The Backstreet Boys
and Hansen because every generation needs
their Partridge Family. Let there be self esteem
and spellcheck and calculators so that brains become lazy
and believe in Me all the more. Let there be assassinations
and natural disasters and executions and mass suicides
and abortions and plane crashes and nuclear accidents
because my children took that ""Be fruitful and multiply"
    thing
way too seriously. And God said, let there be Satan, so
    people
don't blame everything on me. And let there be lawyers,
    so people
don't blame everything on Satan. Let there be toupees
for the bald with money, and paint for the bald who have
none.

And God said, Let the blind lead the blind, let the deaf
sing to the deaf,
and let the dumb become spokesmodels. Let there be war
and famine and pestilence on CNN in prime time.
Let there be celebrities, and celebrity golf tournaments,
and Celebrity Jeopardy, but make the questions so easy
a dog could answer them. Let there be vegetarians and
vegans
and Romulans and Vulcans and trekkies and moonies
and circus freaks and dominatrixes
and harlots and haberdashers and hooked-on-phonics.
And David Bowie. Let there be David Bowie.
And God said, let's dance.
Let's put on our red shoes and dance the blues.
Let there be art for the starving, pornography for the fat,
and dogs playing poker for everyone else.

And God said, Let My people go.
And God said, let My people come.
Now let them go again.
And the people said, Lord we are confused.
And God said, Don't be confused,
just watch out for the meek, they think
they're going to get it all.

And God said,
Let 'em eat cake.
Let me say this about that.
Let me entertain you.
Let it alone or it'll never heal.
Let your love flow.
Let a smile be your umbrella
on a rainy, rainy day.
Let it out and let it in,
Hey, Jude,
begin.

February 1999,
Tujunga, Calif.

underachiever

Never been
chained to the back of a pickup
and dragged into headlessness.

Wasn't born
in a hotel room
and murdered moments later
by my panicky parents.

Never walked
into the schoolyard
and mowed down my classmates
with a deer rifle.

Never impregnated
my English teacher.

Never done anything
newsworthy.

June 11, 1998
Tujunga, Calif.

the path

Walking through the house
in darkness, this is the chair
my sudden foot has found before.
Step slowly, through the air
as still as ever now. The women
asleep, their tiny bodies thrown
about the beds. Turning
out lights and checking doors. Alone
I seek the black silence, where nothing
comes as easily as something.

The unstrung piano, tuneless guitar
loll against white walls, the street
lights and headlamps of cars convey
the odd shadows of no one. The beat
of moccasin footsteps, the clock like
an old faucet. This is time leaking
its way out of me. Closing my eyes,
somewhere I hear my parents, speaking
about me, worried. The fireplace full
of ashes. The path is all memory.

February 17-20, 1999
Tujunga, Calif.

new test

This new test
of strength becomes
how to write notpoems
that make money
to feed and clothe
those in my care.

Is being
aimlessly sober
better than fixatedly
drunk on your own
ability?

A one-legged man
crutches by,
reminding me.

October 26, 1998
Mexico City

lately

(For Phil Hall)

Lately I've been reading your poems.

Wondering what it is that draws me
so deeply inside them.

Wondering even if I'll ever get out.
Back to my own.

The church taught me guilt
how not to listen
and how to lie and live with it.

The town taught me
not to ride a bicycle
with a poem in my head.

University taught me the truth
of ambiguity. That activities
to some are beliefs to others.

The stage taught me quickness
of tongue, the pure reality
of failure.

I have lived all along with only language
and its sound.

I go exploring in your word-caves,
my ears awake,
a light strapped to my head,

June 13-15, 1998
Tujunga, Calif.

aqualung

In the pool of my dreams
there is a child I swim with,
a fish child, gilled and smiling,
fin-footed and scaled with a human head.

My child.

She lives in the pool I can only afford
in my dreams.

I dream that I awaken
and rush out to make sure
she hasn't drowned,
and she leaps assuredly into my arms,
the hump on her back growing,
the blowhole making diapers unnecessary.

And we swim, splashing and laughing,
until I am tired and must rest.
And the hands she grows
out of her fins seem unusually large.

When I falter she swims away,
strong and sure in the lapping water,
calling to me in a language
I will never speak or truly understand.

May 4, 1999
Tujunga, Calif.

humerus

Poetry's elbow
bends to its point,
searching for someone
to nudge.

Hey, look over here,
now over there,
now just keep looking.

Longboats pushed
out of second floor windows,
full of heirlooms
and fear.

Thanks for the ditch
that saved the town.

Thanks for the memory
failing to drown.

Thanks for the soup
in the hollowed-out loaf
with the slam-poet
that night in Vancouver.

The flood,
the long march to somewhere
that resembles death,
the wet, glistening night.

Poetry's elbow
digging into the rib collective.
A reminder to see
things as they aren't.

May 18-June 9, 1998
Toronto-Tujunga

post-convivial

Bent elbow philosophy
poured liberally
over a faux-oak bar.
Ash finger-flicked
unerringly into a black tray
serving as punctuation.

The story is taken
in long draughts without breath.
Unsipped, unsavored,
impatient.

Surrounded by slurred
synervous image-illogic,
you don't notice
the woman sitting over there,
trying to catch your eye in her hand.

You're studying his face.
An imagined nation of insult
injury, lexicon of unluck,
blasphemy, regret.

And the soaked words spill
in some torchsong order,
a rainbow of crossed veins.

The crushed cigarette signals.
You realize it's time
to nod knowingly.

His sigh makes the room
seem empty. The peripherous
woman smiles to herself.
Dismissed with two waves
you make lame goodnights.

And are outside in the air
before realizing the facts
are still stuck to your fingers.

April 24-May 10, 1998
Vancouver-Los Angeles

the idea of falling

Asleep to truth,
yet awake to the odor
of my dream. The perfect
smell of smoke and illicit
behaviour. And I take
the cigarette, a hand-rolled skunk,
in one hand, the bottle fisted
in the other, as the room shrinks
and my lungs cry out for clear skies.

There is a closet
in the insanitarium
where I am still hiding.
It has a window that looks down
on a river that rushes
to somewhere else. Unconscious
to movement, I want to jump
and float with the current,
any current, as long as
I'm not in control.

Of course we cannot even bathe
in the river. It is foul, our keepers
tell us, polluted with bad memories.
Yet we hear it calling all night
as it moves on, forgetting
the shape of sharp stones.

I break the window at long last
and awaken, desperate,
tasting the information on my tongue.
Realizing it was only
the *idea* of falling, and grateful
for the blessing of another day
on the ledge.

May 20, 1999
Tujunga, Calif.

stone cast

Fat with temper,
I struggle for a kind tone
to the voice infused
with breathsucking.

Talked aloud all the way
home in the car
to no one.

My summation –
the I'm right and you're
wrong of my life – still
dribbles out of me
like pus.

Actually thinking,
he'll understand. He'll
see at last how right
I've been all this time.

And through the screendoor,
from the blackness of late
becoming early, comes
that odd high sound.
Circling my head, searching
for the good ear.

The wheezechuckle,
the unstopped psychotic hilarity
of the sure.

Sure the way a man dying
from a shark attack knows
it's the blood's fault.

May 11, 1999
Tujunga, Calif.

lost boy

I am staring at a Utrillo street.
I've been standing here a long time.

If you come searching,
you might not even stop
to look here.

It is just a street.
A white wall,
a tree,
a road that turns to the left
and is gone,
under small pieces of sky.

And each time my eyes move,
another colour of truth emerges
until all I am sure of is there
on the narrow brown cobblestone
that turns left under
small pieces of sky.

If I am gone
when you come, look down
the painted street as far
and as long as you can,
until you are frightened
and completely alone.

October 4, 1999
Off Baja, Calif.